Clayton Colman Hall

The Great Seal of Maryland

A Paper read Before the Maryland Historical Society

Clayton Colman Hall

The Great Seal of Maryland
A Paper read Before the Maryland Historical Society

ISBN/EAN: 9783337416980

Printed in Europe, USA, Canada, Australia, Japan

Cover: Foto ©ninafisch / pixelio.de

More available books at **www.hansebooks.com**

Fund-Publication, No. 23.

THE

Great Seal of Maryland;

A Paper read before the Maryland Historical Society,

December 14, 1885,

BY

CLAYTON C. HALL,

A MEMBER OF THE SOCIETY.

Baltimore, 1886.

PEABODY PUBLICATION FUND.

COMMITTEE ON PUBLICATION.

1886.

JOHN W. M. LEE,
BRADLEY T. JOHNSON,
HENRY STOCKBRIDGE.

PRINTED BY JOHN MURPHY & CO.
PRINTERS TO THE MARYLAND HISTORICAL SOCIETY,
BALTIMORE, 1886.

TO THE

HONORABLE JOHN H. B. LATROBE,

President of the Maryland Historical Society,

THE FOLLOWING BRIEF CONTRIBUTION TO MARYLAND'S HISTORY

IS RESPECTFULLY INSCRIBED

BY THE AUTHOR.

ACKNOWLEDGMENT.

In collecting the material for this paper, much of which was derived from manuscript records hitherto unpublished, the writer has received very kind assistance for which he desires to express his grateful acknowledgments. Especially are they due to Spencer C. Jones, Esq., Clerk of the Court of Appeals of Maryland, for examining and comparing seals attached to original copies of laws in his custody; to J. Thomas Scharf, Esq., Commissioner of the Land Office of Maryland, for facilities extended for searching the records in the Land Office, and to George H. Shafer, Esq., Chief Clerk of the Land Office, for assistance most courteously given, in gaining access to and examining old books and documents. The writer's thanks are also due to Stephen Tucker, Esq., of London, Somerset Herald, and to Dr. William Hand Browne, Librarian of the Johns Hopkins University, for valuable suggestions.

THE GREAT SEAL OF MARYLAND.

THE Great Seal of Maryland presents a marked contrast to those of the other States of the American Union in that its device consists of armorial bearings of a strictly heraldic character, being in fact the family arms of the Lords Baltimore which were placed by the first Proprietary upon the Seal of the Province at the time of its founding.

Most of the States have upon their seals emblems indicative of agriculture and commerce, plenty and prosperity, or kindred subjects, represented in a more or less pictorial or allegorical manner. The colonies that were governed directly under the British Crown formerly had seals upon which were symbols of the royal authority; but these were discarded at the time of the Revolution, and in their stead were adopted devices more in harmony with the new order of affairs. The New England Colony and Virginia, for example, had seals bearing upon

9

the obverse the effigy of the sovereign and upon the reverse the royal arms of Great Britain. The Seal of Carolina had depicted on one side horns of plenty and other symbols of a youthful colony, and upon the other the arms of the eight Lords Proprietors. But this seal like those of the royal colonies, has become a thing of the past.[1]

Maryland, like the other States, put aside shortly after the Revolution the seal in use during the colonial period and adopted one supposed to be more in consonance with the spirit of republican institutions; but after a while the historic interest attaching to the old Provincial Seal came to be recognized, and the ancient coat-of-arms was finally, by legislative enactment, restored to the Seal of the State. Interest in the subject has lately been revived by the discovery at Annapolis of the old seal used under the Proprietary government of the Lords Baltimore, which was believed to have been long ago destroyed. It is safe to say that the old silver seal thus recently brought to light is the

[1] To the Seal of New York adopted in 1778, and re-established by legislative enactment in 1882, an historic origin is ascribed. In 1687, a seal, which continued in use for less than one year, was sent to the Province by James II., and in the warrant by which it was accompanied, it was described as bearing "the effigy of the King on horseback in arms, over a landscape of land and sea with a rising sun." The rising sun and the landscape appear upon the present Seal of that State. The probable origin of this device was discussed in a paper entitled "The Correct Arms of the State of New York," read before the Albany Institute, May 24, 1881, by Henry A. Homes, LL. D., Librarian of the State Library.

most interesting, if not the oldest relic of the kind
in this country.

The object of this paper is to trace, as far as the
materials for the purpose have been found, the
history of Maryland's seal, the several changes
that have at different times been made in it, and
the circumstances by which those changes have
been occasioned.

The subject, so far as it relates to the early
seals, possesses now an antiquarian interest only;
but two centuries ago strong associations clung
to a Great Seal as a symbol of authority and
an important instrument in the exercise of government. This fact is illustrated by an incident
mentioned by Lord Macaulay in his History of
England. He tells that when James II. fled
from his kingdom he sought to bring upon the
country the evils of anarchy, and as a means to
that end he destroyed the writs that had been
prepared for a new Parliament, and taking with
him in his flight the Great Seal, he flung it into
the Thames near Lambeth. A recent writer has
further illustrated this subject by adopting the
loss of the Great Seal of England, and the inconveniences and embarrassments resulting therefrom,
as the basis for the incidents of a story. In Maryland under the Proprietary government all grants
of land were made by or in the name of the Lord
Proprietary and authenticated by the Great Seal

of the Province, which was therefore an object of
great importance both to the Proprietary himself
and to the land holders. That Lord Baltimore so
regarded it is shown by the fact that in sending a
new seal, in 1648, for use in Maryland in place of
one that had been lost, he expressed as his motive
for so doing that it was " necessary for the better
government of our said Province, and satisfaction
of the people there, to have a seal of ours constantly remaining in the said Province and appropriated thereunto and known to be our Great Seal
of the same."

The seal just referred to, which was sent to the
Province by Cecilius Lord Baltimore, by the hands
of Captain William Stone, is the first Great Seal of
Maryland of which there is a recorded description.
This seal was sent to replace one which having been
stolen in 1644, during the rebellion of Richard
Ingle, was subsequently lost or destroyed; and a
minute description of it is contained in the letter of
commission,[1] dated August 12th, 1648, by which it
was accompanied. No impressions of the first Great
Seal, which was in use only during the brief period
intervening between the date of the settlement of
the colony and the year 1644, can be found. Its
exact device is therefore unknown. The seal of
1648 was, however, described by the Lord Proprietary as differing but little from its predecessor.

[1] Commission for the Great Seal; see Appendix, Note A.

In 1652, four years after the sending out of the
second seal, it, with the government of the Province passed into the hands of Commissioners
appointed by Parliament; and it was not until
March 24th, 1657–8, that the Lord Proprietary's
authority was re-established. In November, 1657,
in anticipation of the restoration of his authority,
negotiations for which were already in progress,
Lord Baltimore deemed it necessary, in accordance
with his intention previously expressed in letters
the record of which has been preserved,[1] to provide
a third Great Seal for the Province. Of this
third seal, which was sent to the Province in the
charge of Captain Josias Fendall, no description
was given; but in the letter of instructions which
accompanied it authority was given to Fendall,
who was appointed " Lieutenant and Keeper of the
Great Seal," to pass grants in his Lordship's name
under the new seal, and particular directions were
given, in relation to a certain grant that had been
promised, that if no record could be found of its
having been passed under the former seal, then the
grant was to be made under the new one.[2]

It is, perhaps, impossible now to determine
which seal remained subsequently in use in the
Province. It would be natural to conclude that it

[1] Archives of Maryland; Proceedings of the Council, 1636–1667, pp. 325,
329.
[2] Ibid., p. 335.

must have been the third one sent out in 1657; but it is by no means certain that such was the case, and for some reasons it appears probable that the seal of 1648 was continued in use.

In the articles of agreement arranged between the Proprietary and the Commissioners for the restoration of the former's authority, it was stipulated that the "people in opposition" should deliver up to his Lordship's Governor or Secretary all records of the Province then in their power, and also his Lordship's former Great Seal of the Province "if it be to be found or procured by them."[1] And in pursuance of the instructions given him, Governor Fendall, at a conference with the Commissioners, read the articles of agreement and demanded the records, Great Seal and the whole government to be resigned up into his hands.[2] After some debate and amendment of the articles, they were, on the second day thereafter, March 24th, "read fair engrossed on parchment to the Commissioners, and being to the peace of all parties, were by the Governor and Secretary signed, and afterwards in the face of the people sealed."[3]

If Governor Fendall's demand for the surrender of the former Great Seal was complied with as well as his demand for the surrender of the government, it seems not unlikely that he may have

<hr/>

[1] Ibid., p. 333.   [2] Ibid., p. 335.   [3] Ibid., p. 340.

continued the old seal in use. At all events it appears to have been used by his immediate successors. There are now extant, attached to ancient grants and patents, many impressions of the Great Seal used after this date, and they are in exact accord with the elaborate and minute description given of the seal of 1648; so that if they were made from the seal of 1657, it must be concluded that the latter was a duplicate of the former, or else that the difference between the two was so slight that the written description serves equally well for either.

It seems improbable that the new seal should so closely resemble the old; for if the latter were in existence, but could not be recovered, its fraudulent use in the hands of unauthorized persons would have needed to be specially guarded against, and this would require that the impressions of the new seal should be clearly distinguishable from those of the old. Furthermore, Thomas Bacon, the careful and accurate compiler of the laws of Maryland, while noting in the preface to his compilation, published in 1765, the several occasions upon which portions of the early records had been lost, speaks of the loss of records and the Great Seal during the Ingle rebellion. "The Great Seal," he says, "was never found," and adds, that the one by which it was replaced in 1648, is "the same which is in use at present." That he did not

write in ignorance or forgetfulness of the seal sent
out nine years later is shown by his reference in
the very next paragraph to Lord Baltimore's letter,
written in November, 1657, and to the surrender of
the government by Cromwell's Commissioners to
Josias Fendall, the newly commissioned Lieutenant
General. "It is more than probable," Bacon
remarks, alluding to the time during which the
Proprietary's authority was in abeyance, "that
many records were lost or destroyed in this
unsettled period;" but he makes no suggestion
as to the loss of the seal at this time.

The question as to which of the two was the one
subsequently in use could only be settled definitely
by the discovery of a patent or other document to
which the Great Seal had been affixed between the
years 1648 and 1652, so that the comparison with
impressions of later date could be made. No such
paper has yet been found. But whichever it was,
Lord Baltimore's description of the seal of 1648
affords an adequate description of the one actually
in use from this time on during the continuance
of the Proprietary government.

On the obverse of this seal was the equestrian
figure of the Lord Proprietary, symbolizing his
personal authority. He was represented arrayed
in complete armor, and bearing a drawn sword
in his hand. The caparisons of the horse were
adorned with the family coat-of-arms. On the

[REVERSE.]

[OBVERSE.]

THE GREAT SEAL OF MARYLAND:

UNDER THE PROPRIETARY GOVERNMENT OF THE LORDS BALTIMORE.

ground below were represented some flowers and grass growing. The entire figure was admirably designed and full of life. On the circle surrounding this side of the seal was the inscription, *Caecilius Absolutus Dominus Terrae Mariae et Avaloniae Baro de Baltemore.*

On the other, or reverse, side of the seal was Lord Baltimore's hereditary coat-of-arms. The first and fourth quarters represented the arms of the Calvert family, described in heraldic language as paly of six pieces, or and sable, a bend counterchanged. The second and third quarters showed the arms of the Crossland family which Cecilius inherited from his grandmother, Alicia, daughter of John Crossland, Esquire, of Crossland, Yorkshire, and wife of Leonard Calvert, the father of George, first Lord Baltimore. This coat is quarterly, argent and gules, a cross bottony counterchanged. Above the shield was placed an earl's coronet; above that a helmet set full faced; and over that the Calvert crest, two pennons, the dexter or, the other sable, staves gules, issuing from a ducal coronet. The supporters upon this seal were a plowman and a fisherman, designated respectively by a spade and a fish held in the hand. The motto was that adopted by the Calvert family,—*Fatti maschi parole femine.* Behind and surrounding both shield and supporters was depicted an ermine-lined mantle; and on the circle about this side of

3

the seal were the words *Scuto bonae voluntatis
tuae coronasti nos.* In them will be recognized a
part of the last verse of the Fifth Psalm, as it
appears in the Vulgate;[1] but it may reasonably be
doubted whether the selection of this verse by
Lord Baltimore was not due as much to his
appreciation of the "good will" of his Royal
Master, to which he owed his "coronet," as to
his piety.

The arms thus described have become the historic Arms of Maryland. It is therefore of interest
to consider them somewhat minutely. The meaning
or significance of heraldic devices is generally difficult to trace. Derived, probably, in their simpler
forms, from the usual methods of strengthening or
adorning shields, they soon came to be availed of as
a means of identification on the field of battle. It
was therefore not unusual to select devices which
would convey a suggestion of the bearer's name, or
an allusion to some exploit by which he was distinguished. Heralds of a later date than the age
of chivalry exercised their ingenuity in discovering
or inventing interpretations for the various figures
and "ordinaries" of heraldry. While the mean-
ings ascribed to them by these writers were, many
of them, purely fanciful, they were at the same
time ingenious, and often graceful. But whether

---

[1] The rendering in the Authorized English Version is "With favor wilt
thou compass him as with a shield." Marginal reading: "Crown him."

the interpretation assigned to a particular device or figure as its original meaning, be in itself war‑ rantable or not, it is not to be assumed that the mere fact of bearing the device upon a coat‑of‑ arms involves a reference to the exploit or quality which it may in other cases have been used to commemorate.

According to the commentators upon heraldry [1] the six vertical pieces (or pales), into which the Calvert shield is divided would represent palings or palisades, and constitute the heraldic symbol of a stockade or fortification, which would be appro‑ priate to one who had fortified a town or success‑ fully stormed a hostile fort. The diagonal band, or bend, was held to represent either a sword‑belt or a scaling‑ladder. Taken in connection with the pales the latter meaning would more naturally be ascribed to it. [2]

[1] The principal works to which reference has been made for the meaning ascribed to heraldic figures and the definition of terms are Guillim's Dis‑ play of Heraldry and Edmondson's Complete Body of Heraldry.

[2] The Calvert family was of Flemish origin, and the arms above described are in fact of modern date. The writer is informed, though the courtesy of Stephen Tucker, Esq., of London, Somerset Herald, that they were assigned to Sir George Calvert (afterwards first Baron of Baltimore), by Sir Richard St. George, Knt., Norroy King of Arms, on November 30, 1622. Sir George Calvert was said to be descended from "a noble and ancient family of Flanders;"—but the arms of that family were described as "Or, three mart‑ lets sable." The colors alone of the Flemish arms were preserved in those borne in England. It has been suggested that the pales and bend of the Calvert arms represented the warp and woof of a woven fabric, or a loom traversed by a shuttle, in allusion to the Flemish industry of weaving. But

The Crossland arms present a cross upon a quarterly field. The relation between name and arms is sufficiently obvious. A quarterly field was said to represent a shield broken in battle, indicating that its bearer had proved himself valiant in fight. The cross was held in general to be the symbol of the Christian warrior, and especially appropriate to such as had been Crusaders. Particular significance was also attached to the various forms in which the cross was represented. The bottony or *budding* cross depicted upon these arms was said to represent the budding virtues of a youthful champion.[1] The Crossland arms are generally described as bearing a flory cross, the ends of which are open and expanded like the upper half of a fleur-de-lis. This form differs but little in appearance from the cross bottony, and was described as representing in their full *flower* and development those virtues which the latter indicated as being in their *bud* and promise.[2]

The combination of the Calvert and Crossland arms upon one shield presents an effect of special

this theory appears to be as difficult of substantiation as some of the less prosaic interpretations derived from the mediæval heralds. See remarks of Mr. Frank B. Mayer upon the Maryland Coat-of-Arms, in Baltimore *Sun*, June 17, 1882.

[1] Newton's Display of Heraldry, (London, 1846.)

[2] The date of the Crossland arms is not given. They were recognized as pertaining to the family (which is itself traced back to the time of Edward I.) in the Heralds' Visitation of 1663. The bottony cross was sometimes known as *trefflée* from the resemblance of its terminals to trefoils, and was hence regarded as conveying an allusion to the Holy Trinity.

symmetry. Each consists of a party-colored field, upon which is a single figure, with simply the colors of the field transposed or counterchanged. The parallel lines and acute angles of the one coat are offset by the rectangular arrangement and curves which appear in the other; while the sombre effect of the gold and black is contrasted by the brilliancy of the silver and red.

The pennons which form the crest are such as were commonly attached to spears and lances. They display the Calvert colors—gold and black. The ducal coronet above which they appear takes the place merely of the *torce* or twisted wreath upon which crests ordinarily are placed; but the substitution of a coronet in this place was regarded as an honorable distinction.

The earl's coronet by which the shield was surmounted was borne by the Lords Baltimore only in relation to their American Province, to which was accorded by royal charter the rank of a County Palatine.[1] The rank of a Count Palatine is held to

---

[1] Charter of Maryland. Patent Roll. 8 Charles I. Part 3. No. 2594. Archives of Maryland; Proceedings of the Council, 1636–1667, p. 4. The language of the charter is as follows: "Cum omnibus et singulis hujusmodi ac adeo amplis juribus jurisdiccionibus privilegiis Prerogativis regalitatibus libertatibus immunitatibus juribusque regalibus et Franchesiis quibuscunque temporalibus tam per mare quam per terram infra regionem Insulas Insululas et limites predictos Habendum exercendum utendum et gaudendum prout aliquis Episcopus Dunelmensis infra Episcopatum sive Comitatum Palatinum Dunelmensem in Regno nostro Anglie unquam antehac habuit tenuit usus vel gavisus fuit seu de jure habere tenere uti vel gaudere debuit aut potuit."

be equivalent to that of an Earl, and though the
Norman title of Count or *Comes* did not supplant
in England the Saxon designation Earl or *Eorl*,
Countess became and is now the title of an Earl's
wife. The coronet on the seal was represented as
spanned by an arch and surmounted by a mound
and cross, emblems of sovereign authority.

The position of the helmet, placed full faced,
indicates the exercise of government, by an absolute jurisdiction, over a free state or country. The
helmet of a count palatine would not be mistaken,
even when thus placed, for a royal helmet, as the
latter is represented in heraldry as of gold, and the
former of steel.

In England, and in relation to his rank as an
Irish Peer, Lord Baltimore could only bear the
baron's coronet[1] and the helmet in profile. This
position of the helmet indicates feudal allegiance,
as though the bearer looked, not to the front in
his own right, but toward his liege.

The supporters, a plowman and a fisherman,
evidently represent colonists, and the allusion was
no doubt intended to Maryland's resources in agri-

[1] Lord Baltimore described the coronet on the seal as a Count Palatine's
Cap. According to Edmondson, the privilege of wearing coronets was not
granted to Barons until the reign of Charles II. Originally the Barons
were distinguished by a crimson cap turned up with white fur. (Edmondson's Complete Body of Heraldry, Vol. I, p. 198.) The same writer states
that the right to wear coronets was accorded to Earls in the time of
Henry III.

culture and fisheries. The supporters proper to Lord Baltimore's family arms were leopards, in whose tawny and spotted hides were repeated the tinctures of the Calvert shield.

The motto *Fatti maschi parole femine* is an ancient Italian proverb which early found its way into England. George Herbert in the *Jacula Prudentum* gives the rendering "Words are women, deeds are men." It is stated, on the authority of the distinguished Oriental scholar, Sir William Jones, that a similar saying is found in India, in the form "Words are the daughters of earth, deeds are the sons of heaven."[1]

The antithesis resulting from the genders of the Italian nouns is necessarily lost in translation. One or two English versions have been suggested which do some violence, perhaps, to the sense originally intended,[2] but possibly only to improve it. The most graceful, if not the most accurate of these is "Manly Deeds, Womanly Words." The alliterative expression "Courage and Courtesy"

---

[1] See Bartlett's "Familiar Quotations."

[2] The true significance of this proverb, as explained in the Italian Dictionaries, is simply that deeds are of more avail than words. This is expressed in the *Vocabolorio Italiano della Lingua Parlata* (*Rigutini e Fanfani*), by the following comment: "Come i maschi si reputano più operosi e forti delle femmine, così per dire che i fatti approdano più delle parole suol dirsi che *I fatti son maschi e le parole son femmine.*" The meaning of the proverb is remarked upon by Dr. Wm. Hand Browne in "Maryland: The History of a Palatinate," page 67, note.

has also been suggested, but this is a happy para-
phrase and not a rendering of the original.

Such was the Great Seal of Maryland under the
Proprietary government of the Lords Baltimore.
From grants given under it the titles to most of
the lands in Maryland are ultimately derived, and
several families whose ancestors were among the
early settlers, hold their estates to-day immedi-
ately under such a grant without a single other
conveyance having intervened.

During the sway of the Royal Governors, from
1692 to 1715, while the jurisdiction of the Pro-
prietaries was superseded by the Crown, other
seals came into use. The first of these was
frequently designated in the papers to which it
was affixed as the *Broad* Seal of the Province.
This seal was formally adopted by the Council at a meeting held at the City of St. Mary's, on
the first day of October, 1692, Lionel Copley, Esq.,
being Governor. But this action was not taken
without the direct sanction of royal authority; for,
as the record[1] shows, " His Majesty's Warrant
dated the 7th day of January, Anno Domini 1691–2
for making use of the new Broad Seal appointed
for this Province " was first " produced and read."
No description of this seal was entered on the
minutes at this time, and no impression from it
has been found. The royal warrant above quoted

---

[1] Proceedings of the Council, Liber K., 1692–1694, fol. 47.

has however been preserved in the Public Record Office in London, and it contains a full description of the seal.[1] Upon the obverse were the royal arms of England with this inscription upon the border: *Gulielmus III. et Maria II. Dei Gratia Mag. Brit. Fran. et Hiber. Rex et Regina Fidei Defensores.* On the reverse was the royal cypher, surmounted by a crown, and these words upon the circumference: *Sigillum Provinciae de Maryland in America.*

This seal continued in use until 1706, four years after the accession of Queen Anne to the throne of England, when it was returned to that country by the hands of Evan Evans, to be delivered by Col. Nathaniel Blakiston, agent for the Province, to the Lords of Trade and Plantations.[2]

The seal next in use appears to have been adopted with scant formality. Among the proceedings at a meeting of the Council, held September 22d, 1706, the following entry appears: "The Seals for Govern^r & Councill Provinciall Court & Twelve Countys were brought by Mr. Evan Thomas & well approved off, and Ordered that he be allowed forty shilling for each Seale to be paid by the publiq & recommended to the Comittee for allowance.

"Also Order that the s̄d Seals be used in ye Councill Prov^{ll} & County Courts."

---

[1] See Appendix, Note B.

[2] Proceedings of the Council, Liber C. B., 1704–1708, fol. 56.

Then follows a record of the return of the previous seal to England, and a copy of the receipt
given to the Governor, John Seymour, by Mr.
Evans, when it was committed to his custody. In
this receipt the seal is designated as "two pieces
of silver plate," engraved in the manner already
described, and formerly "used as the Great Seal of
the Province." [1]

In less than a year after the accession of George
I. the government of the Province was restored to
the Proprietary. The title was then vested in
Charles, fifth Baron of Baltimore, a minor, for
whom Lord Guilford was guardian. The old seal
now once more became the Great Seal of the Province. The first document to which it was affixed
after this restoration was a proclamation issued by
the Governor, John Hart, who having held office
under the Crown was re-commissioned as Governor
for the Proprietary. This proclamation, dated
December 27th, 1715, and attested by "his Lordship's Great Seale" was issued to dissolve the General Assembly for the reason that having been
called "by his Majesty's writs of election," it would
not be proper for them to meet and enact laws in
the Proprietary's name. [2]

The territorial rights of the Lords Baltimore had
been respected during the period of royal interven-

---

[1] See Appendix, Note B.
[2] Proceedings of the Council, Liber C. B., 1714–1715.

tion in the government. They were still recognized as "lords of the soil," and made grants of lands to which the old seal was affixed. It was, however, designated in these grants merely as the Proprietary's "Greater Seal at Arms."[1]

In a law that was passed shortly after this time[2] providing for the punishment of counterfeiters of the official seals in use in the Province, the Great Seal is given both the designations by which it had then become known, being called in the title of the law "the Lord Proprietary's Greater Seal at Arms," but in the text, "the Great Seal of the Province."

There were several lesser seals in use under the Proprietary government, and impressions of some of them have been preserved. Among the Archives of Maryland there is a copy of laws enacted by the General Assembly between the years 1642 and 1678, which is attested by the signature of William Calvert, Secretary, and with the signature is affixed an oval seal,[3] about one inch and a quarter in length, containing the quarterly coat-of-arms as upon the Great Seal, but with the leopards, already referred to, as supporters. The count palatine's coronet does not appear on this seal.

[1] A seal affixed to some of the documents, commissions, &c., signed by the Proprietary himself in England was similarly designated.

[2] Acts of 1717, Chapter 8.

[3] Liber W. H. & L., Part W. H., fol. 182.

An impression of the same seal is affixed to a warrant for re-survey issued to the surveyor of Talbot County, in the name of Charles, Lord Baltimore, under date of October 16th, 1713.[1] This warrant is signed by Charles Carroll, and the seal is described in the instrument as " his Lordship's lesser seal at arms." It was apparently the one kept in the Province for the use of the Secretary.[2]

Papers executed in England under the Proprietary's own hand were frequently authenticated by a seal also described as the " lesser seal at arms." An impression of the one used by Frederick, Lord Baltimore, is attached to the commission of Hugh Hammersley as Secretary of the Province, dated November 4th, 1765.[1] This seal has upon it the quarterly coat and the count palatine's coronet. The supporters are a plowman and a fisherman as upon the Great Seal, but they are transposed, the fisherman being upon the right and the plowman on the left. The pennons which form the crest are also reversed, being made to flow toward the dexter side.[3] This seal is of nearly the same size as the one just described.

[1] Preserved in the Library of the Maryland Historical Society.

[2] This seal, which is made of silver, was among those recently discovered at Annapolis. See page 39.

[3] Pennons and flags when used in heraldry are usually made to flow toward the sinister, as though being borne to the right, the direction in which helmets when represented in profile are made to face. In the illustration of Lord Baltimore's arms printed in Guillim's Display of

In the Land Office at Annapolis there is an agreement, dated July 4th, 1760, between Frederick, Lord Baltimore, and Thomas and Richard Penn, sons and heirs of William Penn, touching the boundary between Maryland and Pennsylvania. Lord Baltimore's seal affixed to this agreement is evidently that which pertained to him as Baron of Baltimore. It is nearly square in form, with rounded corners, about one inch in size, and has upon it the Calvert arms only, with a baron's coronet and the leopards as supporters.

A wood-cut showing the arms as they appear upon this seal was printed upon the title page of the laws of Maryland, published between the years 1726 and 1765.

Upon all these small seals a lambrequin attached to the helmet is substituted for the mantle represented upon the Great Seal.[1]

On Sunday, November 3d, 1776, the Convention assembled at Annapolis to devise a form of government for what was now become the State of Maryland, adopted a Declaration of Rights; and on the Friday ensuing, November 8th, the Constitution

Heraldry the pennons are, however, drawn flowing in the opposite direction, as upon the seal above described.

[1] Several of the older counties in Maryland formerly had seals copied from one or other of these smaller seals. Caroline County is the only one that has retained the ancient device. Upon the seal of the Circuit Court for that county still appear the Calvert arms with the supporting leopards.

and Form of Government were agreed to. By the
thirty-sixth article of the Constitution the power to
make the Great Seal of the State was vested in
the Governor's Council, and at a meeting of the
Council held March 31st, 1777, this authority was
exercised by the adoption of an order recorded
among their proceedings as follows :

" The Council being empowered by the Constitution and Form of Government to make the Great
Seal of this State, do make and declare the Great
Seal of Maryland, heretofore used, the Great Seal of
this State, and as such to be used in future until a
new one can be devised and executed, which cannot
be done for immediate service."[1]

Under the authority of this order of the Council
the seal of the Province was continued in use until
the year 1794. In that year the Council adopted a
new seal. It was made by Thackara & Vallance of
Philadelphia, as is shown by an inscription on the
back of the seal (which is preserved at Annapolis),
as well as by an order of the Council adopted January 8th, 1794, directing the payment to them by the
" Treasurer of the Western Shore " of " one hundred and twenty pounds current money " for the
" metal and engraving." This seal, like its predecessor was affixed pendent to documents. Upon
the obverse was a female figure representing Justice,

---

[1] Proceedings of the Council, 1777-1779.

[REVERSE.]

[OBVERSE.]

holding aloft the scales in her left hand, and in her right an olive branch. Rays of light emanated from behind and surrounded the figure. Below were the *fasces* and an olive branch crossed, and upon the border were graven the words " Great Seal of the State of Maryland." On the reverse side was depicted a tobacco hogshead standing upright, with bundles of leaf tobacco lying thereon. Two sheaves of wheat stood in the foreground, and in the background could be seen a ship approaching shore, with fore and main top-sails set, the other sails furled. At the base was a cornucopia. On the circle about this side were the words "Industry the Means and Plenty the Result."

This seal was formally adopted by the Council on February 5th, 1794, and a proclamation, publishing the fact of its adoption, was issued by the Governor. The following entry appears upon the record of the Council Proceedings of that date.[1]

"Whereas it is provided by the 36th Section of the Constitution and Form of Government that 'The Council shall have power to make the Great Seal of this State, which shall be kept by the Chancellor and affixed to all Laws, Commissions, Grants, and other Testimonials as has been heretofore practised in this State,' and Whereas under and in virtue of the said power the Board have lately caused to be

[1] Proceedings of the Council, 1794–1799.

made of silver a great Seal dependent, with certain devices, and with the words 'Great Seal of the State of Maryland' inscribed on one side thereof; and the words 'Industry the Means, and Plenty the Result' on the other, therefore, Ordered That the same be delivered to the Honourable the Chancellor as the Great Seal of this State; and that the same and none other be thereafter kept, used, taken and considered in all respects and to every intent and purpose as the Great Seal of the State of Maryland.

"Ordered, That the Chancellor be requested to deliver to His Excellency the Governor the old Great Seal of this State; and that the same be lodged and safely kept in the Treasury of the Western Shore."

"The following proclamation was issued:

"Whereas &c⁾ . . . as in the foregoing entry, to the end of the preamble; . . . . then as follows.

"And Whereas the Same hath been delivered to the Honble the Chancellor to be kept and used as the Great Seal of this State, I have therefore thought proper to issue this my Proclamation, declaring the seal so as aforesaid made and delivered to the Chancellor, and none other, to be the Great Seal of the State of Maryland.

"Given at Annapolis &c⁾ &c⁾

(Signed) "Thoˢ S. Lee."

This seal continued in use only for twenty-three years. Its size, three and a half inches in diameter, and its pendent form were probably deemed inconveniences; for it was superseded by a much smaller one, which was made, as have been the subsequent seals, to be used with a press and stamped in the papers to which it was affixed.

The order for the new seal is recorded by the following entry among the Council Proceedings under date of March 14th, 1817.[1]

"Ordered that the Great Seal of the State be altered and changed and that the Register in Chancery cause a new seal to be made of the diameter of one inch and a quarter, that the device on the same be the Coat of Arms of the United States surrounded with the words 'Seal of the State of Maryland' and that the same when completed shall be and is hereby declared to be the Seal of the State of Maryland."

The seal prepared under this order was engraved on steel. Its device was merely the American Eagle, as the order of Council required, with thirteen stars in a semicircle above, and surrounded by a border ornamented with thirteen points.

The formal adoption of this seal by the Council occurred on June 9th, 1817, and on the following day a proclamation publishing the fact was issued by the Governor, Charles Ridgely of Hampton. The mode of procedure at the adoption of the previous seal was carefully followed on this occasion.[2]

[1] Proceedings of the Council, 1813-1817.
[2] See Appendix, Note C.

5

This rather insignificant seal was used until 1854 when an attempt was made to restore the arms of the State to their place upon the Great Seal. To Governor E. Louis Lowe is due the suggestion from which ultimately resulted the restoration of the ancient arms.

The Council to the Governor, which formally had jurisdiction over the seal, had been abolished in 1837.[1] Governor Lowe therefore brought the subiect to the attention of the General Assembly. In his message to the Legislature, at the session of 1854, he said : " The Great Seal is much worn by long use. I do not think that it is appropriate. It should in my judgment consist of the arms of the State, and not of a device which has no significant relation to its local history. I recommend that another be provided."

In accordance with this recommendation an act was passed by the Legislature[2] providing for the procuring of a new seal bearing " the arms of the State as heretofore known and accepted," and the motto *Crescite et Multiplicamini.* The act required that the new seal should be used on May 1st, 1854, on which day the old seal should be broken.[3] The intention of the Legislature in respect to the res-

---

[1] Acts of 1836, Chapter 197, § 13, passed March 10, 1837.

[2] See Appendix, Note D.

[3] The old seal, defaced as the law directed, was found in November, 1885, and is now preserved in the Land Office in Annapolis.

THE GREAT SEAL OF MARYLAND:

ADOPTED IN 1817.
(DIAMETER 1¾ INCH.)

THE GREAT SEAL OF MARYLAND:

ADOPTED IN 1854.
(DIAMETER 2¼ INCHES.)

toration of the arms of the State was not successfully carried out at this time. In the preparation of the seal recourse was evidently had to a rough wood-cut printed on the title page of Bacon's Laws of Maryland in 1765, and some errors which it contained were reproduced in the seal. For example, the Calvert arms were made paly of five pieces instead of six, and the portions of the cross in the second and third quarters of the shield which are properly red, were represented as black. These departures were not only errors in fact, but they were in violation of the ordinary rules of heraldic drawing and coloring. The errors did not end here. The coronet, helmet, and crest were correctly represented in the wood-cut; but in their stead a spread eagle was placed upon the seal. The story is told that the gentleman,—an officer of the State government at that time,—to whom was entrusted the task of preparing the new seal, deemed it imprudent to restore the coronet, lest the Whigs, then in opposition in the State, should use the circumstance upon the hustings, and by accusing the Democrats of an intention to restore aristocratic institutions, secure their defeat at the next election. He, therefore, of his own motion and for these prudential considerations, disregarded the directions of the act of the Assembly which required the restoration of the arms "as heretofore known," and substituted for the ancient crest the familiar figure of the American Eagle.

This seal was handsomely engraved on brass by Mr. Edward Stabler, of Montgomery County, Maryland. He was, however, in no wise responsible for the errors in the design.

The date at which the motto *Crescite et Multiplicamini*, placed upon this seal, first came into use in Maryland has not been ascertained. It appeared upon the Maryland coins[1] struck in 1659, during the administration of the first Proprietary and shortly after the sending of the *third* seal to the Province; it was upon the wood-cut in Bacon's Laws already referred to, published in 1765, and also upon the paper money issued by the State at the time of the Revolution, as well as upon other papers and publications. The first word of the motto brings to mind the circumstance, mentioned by Bozman,[2] that it was at first intended to call the Province *Crescentia*, but when the charter was presented to the King, Charles I., for his signature, the name was, at his suggestion, changed to Maryland in honor of the Queen, Henrietta Maria. The possibility suggests itself that this motto may have been in use during the earliest days of the colony.

At the session of the Legislature held in 1874, attention having been by that time attracted to the

---

[1] A few specimens of these coins, which are very rare, are preserved in the collection of the Maryland Historical Society.

[2] Bozman's History of Maryland, Vol. I, p. 271.

errors in the existing Great Seal,[1] a joint resolution was adopted directing its correction;[2] but in this resolution reference was made to the wood-cut in Bacon's Laws as the model to which the corrected seal should conform. When it was recognized that the copying of that wood-cut would result in reproducing some of the errors which it was intended to correct, the Governor, James Black Groome, concluded to take no action under the resolution, and brought the matter to the notice of the Legislature in his message at its next session, in 1876. A carefully prepared resolution was then adopted [3] in which was embodied a full description of the arms intended to be restored, so as to guard against the possibility of errors in the future. The restoration of the Italian motto and the legend upon the circle was also directed. In the preparation of this resolution Lord Baltimore's letter of commission for the seal of 1648, and old impressions of the seal itself, were taken as the guides to be followed, and the

[1] The errors in the seal, and the true description of the Arms of Maryland were pointed out in a communication from the writer of this paper which was read before the Maryland Historical Society at its meeting in May, 1871. A remarkably correct drawing of the Provincial Seal was made in 1876 by Miss Davis, daughter of Hon. Allen Bowie Davis of Montgomery County, from indications afforded by old and imperfect impressions. This drawing was engraved and published in 1880.

[2] See Appendix, Note E.

[3] This resolution was adopted chiefly through the efforts of Dr. Lewis H. Steiner, at that time Senator from Frederick County. See Appendix, Note E.

arms upon that seal were distinctly designated as the Arms of Maryland.

It was not until 1880 that the succeeding Governor, John Lee Carroll, reported to the Legislature that the new seal was completed and had "been in use for the last year." From a note addressed by Richard C. Hollyday, Esq., Secretary of State, to the Maryland Historical Society, presenting to the Society the first impression of the new seal, it appears that it was first used February 27th, 1879.

This seal was engraved upon brass, and executed in Paris, under the order of Governor Carroll. It was not attempted, in preparing the new design, to reproduce the style of the old seal; but the directions contained in the resolution were departed from only in the introduction, not inappropriate in itself, of the figures "1632" (the year in which the Charter of Maryland was signed), at the base of the circle.[1] On the new seal the pennons forming the crest are represented flowing toward the dexter side, as upon the lesser seal used by Frederick, Lord Baltimore.[2] There is no inscription upon this seal to indicate that it is the Great Seal of the State, none having been prescribed in the resolution under which it was prepared.

By the adoption of this seal in 1876 the ancient Arms of Maryland were finally restored in their

---

[1] The drawing for this seal was made by R. G. Harper Pennington, Esq.
[2] See page 28 (note 3).

THE GREAT SEAL OF MARYLAND:

integrity to the Great Seal of the State. The equestrian figure upon the obverse of the old seal, which symbolized the personal authority of the Proprietary, ceased to be appropriate after the downfall of the Proprietary government. But the arms upon the reverse side, which had become identified with the Province, and did not change either in form or significance with changing administrations, are retained as the symbol of the State.

In July, 1884, a search was made for historic relics in the vault of the Treasury Building at Annapolis. The search was rewarded by the discovery of several old seals, and among them the Great Seal of the Province.[1]

This seal differs from the description of that sent out by Cecilius Lord Baltimore, only in that the name of CAROLVS appears on the obverse in place of CÆCILIVS. Cecilius was succeeded in the title by his son Charles, third Baron, in 1675. Benedict Leonard, fourth Baron, held the title but a few weeks in 1715, when it passed, upon his death, to his son Charles, fifth Baron, who lived until 1751. So that for three quarters of a century, with but a single brief interruption, Charles was the name of the Proprietary of Maryland. At

---

[1] The search referred to was undertaken at the instance of J. Thomas Scharf, Esq., Commissioner of the Land Office. Besides the seal mentioned above, there were found the Great Seal adopted in 1794, and the lesser seal mentioned on page 28 (note 2).

some time during this period the name *Carolus*
was placed upon the seal, but no record of the date
has been found. As the name occurs only on the
obverse, this change necessitated the alteration or
renewal of one side of the seal only ; and it appears
upon examination that the change was effected by
an alteration merely of the existing seal. The inscription on the obverse is sharp and distinct
throughout, while that on the reverse is much
worn, and in some places nearly worn away, as
though it had been much longer in service. A
careful comparison shows, too, that the letters on
the two circles are slightly different in form, and
that the plane surfaces of the circles have been
finished differently, as though done at different
times. These points of dissimilarity indicate that
the inscription with the name of *Carolus* is of later
date than the rest of the work. This theory is confirmed by a slight depression along the circle on the
obverse as though the metal had been cut away.
There seems, therefore, to be no reason to doubt
that the old seal recently brought to light at
Annapolis is one that was sent out by Cecilius, the
first Proprietary.

Though worn by long service, and battered and
scarred by careless handling, the designs on both
sides of the seal are still clear and distinct and
show the artistic handiwork of a skilled workman.
One or two matters of detail not mentioned in

Lord Baltimore's description, and which the old impressions do not reveal are to be noted. Where the folds of the mantle surrounding the arms show the outside surface, the edges of the coat-of-arms itself appear, as though it were broidered upon the exterior of the mantle. It is also to be observed that a count palatine's coronet, surmounted by mound and cross, encircles the helmet upon the head of the equestrian figure upon the obverse of the seal.[1]

The discovery of this interesting relic of a past era completes as it were a cycle in the history of Maryland's Seal, and the opportunity is afforded to test, by comparison, the accuracy with which the restoration was effected in 1876. The differences between the representations of the arms of Maryland as depicted on the new seal and on the old are found to be only such as result from the different styles of drawing and engraving. In all that is essential the arms are identical. The seal adopted in 1876 is a practical reproduction, though not a fac-simile, of the reverse side of the ancient seal.

[1] An earl's coronet is described as surrounded by eight pearls raised upon as many points. It is now customary with designers and engravers to draw these coronets uniformly with five points showing. When the Maryland Seal was engraved such careful accuracy was not observed. The coronet over the shield on the reverse side shows six points, while that upon the head of the equestrian figure on the obverse shows but four. The coronets are, however, identical in form.

6

The criticism may perhaps be made upon the seal as now used, that a Republic has no right to display the coronet proper to a County Palatine. But to this it may be answered that it is not borne as a symbol of authority or rank in the present, but in commemoration of a past and of a history which now extends over two centuries and a half.

Taken by itself the history of the Great Seal is but a barren narrative, almost wholly comprised in a few brief public documents,—a letter of commission, an order of the Council, an act of the Assembly; but it is to be noted that the changes which are thus recorded are incident to and directly linked with the most important political events that have marked the history of the Commonwealth. From the time of the founding of the colony at St. Mary's under the Proprietary government, every event that has disturbed the established order,—whether it were the lawless outbreak of an insurgent, the intervention of Commissioners appointed by Parliament, or of Governors appointed by the Crown, or the final struggle which resulted in the establishment of American independence,—was accompanied and reflected by some corresponding change or incident relating to the Great Seal, and an explanation of the latter necessarily involves a reference to the former. By the final restoration of the ancient device in our own times, it is proclaimed, that whatever the changes by which its political constitution has been affected, the identity of the Commonwealth has never been destroyed and its continuity remains unbroken.

APPENDIX.

Note A. (*page 12*).

COMMISSION FOR THE GREAT SEAL.

[*Archives of Maryland: Proceedings of the Council*, 1636–1667, pp. 214, 215.]

Cecilius Absolute Lord and Proprietary of the Provinces of Maryland and Avalon Lord Baron of Baltimore &cᵃ to our trusty and well Beloved Lieuᵗ and Council of our said Province of Maryland to all the Inhabitants of the same and all others whom it may Concern Greeting whereas our Great Seal of the said Province of Maryland was Treacherously and Violently taken away from thence by Richard Ingle or his Complices in or about february Anno Domini One thousand six hundred and fourty & four and hath been ever since so disposed of as it cannot be recovered again for us we do therefore hereby protest against all and every act and things whatsoever which hath been Sealed therewith since the fourteenth of Febʳ Anno Domini One thousand six hundred fourty and four or which shall at any time hereafter be Sealed therewith as unlawful and not done by any Legal Authority from us and we do hereby declare all and every the said Acts and things unlawful and Null but because it is necessary for the better Government of our said Province and Satisfaction of the People there to have a Seal of ours Constantly remaining in the said Province and appropriated thereunto and known to be our Great Seal of the same whereby divers publick Acts and Grants of Lands within the said Province may be rati-

45

fied and Confirmed according to such directions Instructions Commissions or warrants as we have or shall from time to time give under our hand and seal at Arms for that purpose therefore we have provided another new Seal for our said Province in the Room and Place of the other which was so taken away from thence as aforesaid which new Seal we have Committed to the Custody of Captain William Stone whom we have Constituted as well our Chancellor and Keeper of the same as our Lieutenant of the said Province till we or our heirs shall signify our Pleasure to the Contrary the manner & form of the s^d new Seal being this (vizt) on the one side thereof is ingraven our Figure in Compleat Armour on Horse Back with our Sword drawn and our Helmett on and a Great Plume of Feathers affixed to it the Horsetrappings furniture and ·Caparisons being adorn'd with the figure of our Paternal Coat of Arms and underneath the Horse a Sea Shoar engraven with Certain Flowers and Grass Growing upon it and this Inscription about that Side of the Seal (vizt) Cecilius Absolutus Dmũs Terrae Mariae et Avaloniae Baro de Baltimore and on the other or Counterside of the said Seal is engraven a Scutcheon wherein our Paternal Coat of Arms to wit six pieces impaled with a Bend dexter Counterchanged quartered with another Coat of Arms belonging to our Family vizt a Cross Buttoned at each end (and also counterchanged) are engraven the whole Scutcheon being Supported with a Fisherman on the one Side and a Plowman on the other standing upon a Scrowl wherein is engraven the motto of our Paternal Court of Arms vizt ffatti Maschij Parole Femine next above the Scutcheon is engraven a Count Palatines Cap and over that a Helmet with the Crest of our Paternal Court of Arms on the Top of it which Crest is a Ducal Crown with two half Bannerets set upright in it Behind the said Scutcheon and Supporters is engraven a large mantle and this inscription is about that side of the Seal vizt Scuto bonæ Voluntatis tuæ Coronasti nos the figure of the Seal is round and it is of the same Bigness that our said former Great Seal was and cut in Silver as the other was the impression of all which in wax is hereunto affixed it being somewhat different (though but little) from our said former Great Seal of the Said Province and we do hereby declare the said new Seal to be from henceforwards our Great Seal of the said Province of Maryland and that we will have it so to be esteeemed and reputed there till we or our heirs shall signify our or their Pleasure to the Contrary Given at Bath under our hand and our said new Great Seal of the Said Province the 12th day of August in the 17th Year of our Dominion over the said Prov^e of Maryland Annoq Dni 1648.

Note B. (*pages* 25, 26).

The following copy of the royal warrant for the adoption of the seal of 1692, was obtained from Mr. W. Noel Sainsbury, of the Public Record Office, London. Mr. Sainsbury writes that though diligent search was made through many volumes of records and correspondence concerning Maryland no impression of the seal described in the warrant could be found.

THE KING'S WARRANT

TO GOV^R COPLEY

to use the Maryland Seal

P. R. O.
Maryland
B. T.
Vol. 8. p. 39.

7 January 169¹/₂

To Our Trusty an Wellbeloved Lionel Copley Esqr Our Captain Generall and Governor in Chief in and over Our Province and Territory of Maryland in America. You will herewith receive a seal, wch we have thought fit to appoint for the use of Our Province of Maryland, the same being Engraven on the one side with Our Royall Arms, with ye Garter, Crowne, Supporters and Motto, and this Inscription round the Cir-

Warrant for
ye Maryland
Scale *ʃ*

cumference, Gulielmus 3ᵈ et Maria 2ᵈ Dej Gratia Mag: Brit: Fran: et Hiber: Rex et Regina Fidei Defensoris &cᵃ. There being on the other side Our Royall Cypher crowned and this Inscription round the Circumference Sigillum Provincie de Maryland in America; which Seal we do hereby Authorize and Direct to be used in Sealing all Patents and Grants, and all publick Acts and Instruments which shall be made and passed in Our Name for Our Service within Our said Province, And that it be to all Intents and purposes of the same force & Validity as any former Seal within Our Said Province, or as any other Seal Whatsoever appointed for the use of any of Our Plantations in America is or hath been. And so we bid you ffarewell. From Our Court at Whitehall the Seaventh day of January 1691, In the Third Year of Our Reign.

By His Maʸˢ Command.

NOTTINGHAM.

The receipt given by Mr. Evan Evans for this seal when it was returned to England, is recorded as follows in the Archives of Maryland. (Liber C. B. 1704–1708, fol. 56.)

"Maryland Towne & ⎱ Memorandum that this Day to witt the Port of Annapolis Ss ⎰ 14ᵗʰ day of August 1706 I received of his Excellency John Seymour Esqʳ Capᵉ Generale and Governʳ in Cheif of this Province two peices of Silver Plate The one Cutt or engraved with the Arms of England & his late Majesty the other with a Cypher Wᵐ & Mary Rex & Reginia heretofore used as the Great Seale of this Province which I Do promise upon my Safe arrivall in England (God willing) to Deliver to Coll Nathaniell Blakiston agent for the Province of Maryland in order to Carry to their Lordshipps the Lords of Trade & Plantations & to take Coll. Blakiston's Receipt therefore.

" EVAN EVANS."

Note C. (*page* 33).

The adoption of the Seal of 1817 is recorded as follows among the Proceedings of the Council (Liber 1813–1817) under date of June 9th, 1817.

" Whereas it is provided by the 36th section of the Constitution and Form of Government that the Council have power to make the Great Seal of this state which shall be kept by the Chancellor and affixed to all Laws Commissions Grants and other Testimonials as has been heretofore practised in this State and whereas under and in virtue of the said power The Board have lately caused to be made of steel a Great Seal with certain devices and with the words Seal of the State of Maryland to be inscribed thereon and that the same and none other thereafter be kept taken and considered in all respects and to every intent purpose as the Great Seal of the State of Maryland Ordered that the Chancellor be requested to deliver to his Excellency the Governor the Old Great Seal of this State, and that the same be lodged and safely kept in the Treasury of the Western Shore. The following Proclamation issued.

" By His Excellency Charles Ridgely of Hampton Esquire Governor of Maryland

" A Proclamation

" Whereas it is provided by the 36th section of the Constitution and form of Government, that ' the Council shall have power to make the Great Seal of this State which shall be kept by the Chancellor, and affixed to laws commissions grants and other testimonials as has been heretofore practised in this State ' and whereas under and in virtue of the said power, the Board have lately caused to be made of steel a Seal with certain devices and with the words ' Seal of the State of Maryland inscribed thereon. And whereas the same has been delivered to the honourable the Chancellor, to be kept and used as the Great Seal of this State, I have therefore thought proper to issue this my Proclamation declaring the seal so as aforesaid made and delivered to the Chancellor and none other, to be the Great Seal of the State of Maryland. Given under my hand, and the Seal of the State of Maryland this tenth day of June in the year of our Lord one thousand eight hundred and seventeen.

"By His Excellency's Command   "C. RIDGELY of Hampton"
    NINIAN PINKNEY
      Clerk of the Council"

"Ordered that the foregoing Proclamation be published eight times in the Maryland Gazette Federal Gazette, Federal Republican and Telegraph, The Frederick Town Herald, The Torch light, The Allegany Federalist and the Monitor at Easton."

Note D. *(page 34).*

[ACTS OF THE GENERAL ASSEMBLY—1854.]

Chapter 81.

AN ACT to provide for a new Great Seal for this State.

Section 1. Be it enacted by the General Assembly of Maryland, That the Governor be and he is hereby authorized and required to procure a new great seal for this State, the cost of which shall be paid on a Certificate of the Governor by the treasurer, on a warrant from the comptroller.

Sec. 2. And be it enacted, That the seal to be procured shall contain on its face the arms of the State, as heretofore known and accepted, with the motto, in small letters, "Crescite et multiplicamini"; on the upper part of the circle there shall be the words "The Great Seal" and at the bottom, in two horizontal lines, the words, "of Maryland"; the words, "The Great Seal" and "Maryland," to be in large letters; on the left side of the circle, near the bottom, shall be the figures, "1632," and on the right side the figures, "1854"; the diameter of the seal shall be two inches and a quarter.

Sec. 3. And be it enacted, That the new seal shall be used on and after the first day of May next, on which day the Governor shall cause the present seal to be broken.

Sec. 4. And be it enacted, That this act shall take effect on its passage.

(*Passed March* 1, 1854).

Note E. (*page* 37).

The Resolutions adopted by the General Assembly providing for the correction of the Great Seal are as follows :

[JOINT RESOLUTIONS—1874.]

No. 9.

SENATE JOINT RESOLUTION

In relation to the Great Seal of the State.

WHEREAS, certain errors have been made in altering the Great Seal of the State of Maryland; therefore,

Be it resolved by the General Assembly of Maryland, That the Governor of the State is hereby authorized to have the Great Seal of the State so altered as to make it conform to the arms of Lord Baltimore, as represented on the title page of Bacon's Laws of Maryland, printed seventeen hundred and sixty-five, in Annapolis, by Jonas Green.

[JOINT RESOLUTIONS—1876.]

No. 5.

In relation to the Great Seal.

WHEREAS, Senate Joint Resolution, No. nine, " In relation to the Great Seal of the State," passed by the General Assembly, at its session in eighteen hundred and seventy-four, instructing the

Governor to have the Great Seal of the State so altered that it should conform to the arms of Lord Baltimore as represented on the title page of Bacon's Laws of Maryland, printed in seventeen hundred and sixty-five, by Jonas Green, was passed under the impression that the said representation was accurate ; and

WHEREAS, Investigation has shown that said representation of the arms of Lord Baltimore is imperfect; and

WHEREAS, a complete and accurate description of the Seal of the Province is to be found in the commission of Cecilius, Lord Baron of Baltimore, that accompanied the said seal when sent to the Province in sixteen hundred and forty-eight; therefore,

1. *Be it resolved by the General Assembly of Maryland*, That Senate Joint Resolution, No. nine, " In relation to the Great Seal of the State," passed by the General Assembly, at its session in eighteen hundred and seventy-four be, and the same is hereby rescinded.

2. *And be it further resolved*, That the Governor of the State is hereby authorized and empowered to have the Great Seal of the State altered so that it shall bear the arms of Maryland as represented upon the seal furnished the Province in sixteen hundred and forty-eight, by Cecilius, Lord Baron of Baltimore; which arms are described as follows, namely : Quarterly, first and fourth, paly of six or and sable, a bend counterchanged; second and third, quarterly argent and gules, a cross bottony counterchanged ; Crest (which is placed upon a helmet, showing five bars, over a Count-palatine's coronet) on a ducal coronet proper, two pennons, dexter or, the other sable; staves gules; motto " Fatti maschii, parole femine"; supporters, a plowman and a fisherman proper; a mantle doubled with ermine, surrounding the arms and supporters. Upon a border encircling the seal, shall be engraven this legend, " Scuto bonæ voluntatis tuæ coronasti nos." The diameter of the seal shall be three inches.